BRITISH MUNICIPAL BUS OPERATORS

A SNAPSHOT OF THE 1960s

BRITISH MUNICIPAL BUS OPERATORS

A SNAPSHOT OF THE 1960s

JIM BLAKE

Pen & Sword
TRANSPORT

AN IMPRINT OF PEN & SWORD BOOKS LTD.
YORKSHIRE – PHILADELPHIA

First published in Great Britain in 2019 by
Pen and Sword Transport
An imprint of
Pen & Sword Books Ltd
Yorkshire - Philadelphia

ISBN 978 1 47385 718 6

Typeset by Aura Technology and Software Services, India

Printed and bound in India by Replika Press Pvt. Ltd.

Pen & Sword Books Ltd incorporates the Imprints of Pen & Sword Books Archaeology, Atlas, Aviation, Battleground, Discovery, Family History, History, Maritime, Military, Naval, Politics, Railways, Select, Transport, True Crime, Fiction, Frontline Books, Leo Cooper, Praetorian Press, Seaforth Publishing, Wharncliffe and White Owl.

For a complete list of Pen & Sword titles please contact

PEN & SWORD BOOKS LIMITED
47 Church Street, Barnsley, South Yorkshire, S70 2AS, England
E-mail: enquiries@pen-and-sword.co.uk
Website: www.pen-and-sword.co.uk

or

PEN AND SWORD BOOKS
1950 Lawrence Rd, Havertown, PA 19083, USA
E-mail: Uspen-and-sword@casematepublishers.com
Website: www.penandswordbooks.com

CONTENTS

About the Author 6

Introduction 8

Pictures 9

ABOUT THE AUTHOR

I was born at the end of 1947, just five days before the 'Big Four' railway companies, and many bus companies – including London Transport – were nationalised by Clement Attlee's Labour government.

Like most young lads born in the early post-war years, I soon developed a passionate interest in railways, the myriad steam engines still running on Britain's railways in those days in particular. However, because my home in Canonbury Avenue, Islington was just a few minutes' walk from North London's last two tram routes, the 33 in Essex Road and the 35 in Holloway Road and Upper Street, my parents often took me on these for outings to the South Bank, particularly to the Festival of Britain which was held there in the last summer they ran, in 1951. Moreover, my father worked at the GPO's West Central District Office in Holborn and often travelled to and from work on the 35 tram. As a result, he knew many of the tram crews, who would let me stand by the driver at the front of the trams as they travelled through the Kingsway Tram Subway. This was an unforgettable experience for a four-year-old! In addition, my home was in the heart of North London's trolleybus system, with route 611 actually passing the door, and one of the busiest and complicated trolleybus junctions in the world, at Holloway, Nag's Head, a short ride away along Holloway Road. Here, the trolleybuses' overhead almost blotted out the sky! Thus, from a very early age, I developed an equal interest in buses and trolleybuses to that in railways, and have retained both until the present day.

I was educated at my local Highbury County Grammar School, and later at Kingsway College, by coincidence a stone's throw from the old tram subway. I was first bought a camera for my fourteenth birthday at the end of 1961, which was immediately put to good use photographing the last London trolleybuses in North West London on their very snowy last day a week later. Three years later, I started work as an administrator for the old London County Council at County Hall, by coincidence adjacent to the former Festival of Britain site, and travelled to and from work on bus routes 171 or 172, which had replaced the 33 and 35 trams mentioned above.

By now, my interest in buses and trolleybuses had expanded to include those of other operators, and I travelled throughout England and Wales between 1961 and 1968 in pursuit of them, being able to afford to travel further afield after starting work! I also bought a colour cine-camera in 1965, with which I was able to capture what is now very rare footage of long-lost buses, trolleybuses and steam locomotives. Where the latter are concerned, I was one of the initial purchasers of the unique British Railways 'Pacific' locomotive 71000 *Duke of Gloucester*, which was the last ever passenger express engine built for use in Britain. Other preservationists laughed at the group which purchased what in effect was a cannibalised hulk from Barry scrapyard at the end of 1973, but they laughed on the other side of their faces when, after extensive and innovative rebuilding, it steamed again in 1986. It has since become one of the best-known and loved preserved British locomotives, often returning to the main lines.

Although I spent 35 years in local government administration, with the LCC's successor, the Greater London Council, then Haringey Council and finally literally back on my old doorstep, with Islington Council, I also took a break from office drudgery in 1974/75 and actually worked on the buses as a conductor at London Transport's Clapton Garage, on local routes 22, 38 and 253. Working on the latter, a former tram and trolleybus route, in particular was an unforgettable experience! I was recommended for promotion as an inspector, but rightly thought that taking such a job with the surname Blake was unwise in view of the then-current character of the same name and occupation in the *On The Buses* TV series and films, and so declined the offer and returned to County Hall!

By this time, I had begun to have my transport photographs published in various books and magazines featuring buses and railways, and also started off the North London Transport Society, which catered for enthusiasts interested in both subjects. In conjunction with this group, I have also compiled and published a number of books on the subject since 1977, featuring many of the 100,000 or so transport photographs I have taken over the years.

Also through the North London Transport Society, I became involved in setting up and organising various events for transport enthusiasts in 1980, notably the North Weald Bus Rally which the group took over in 1984, and which raised thousands of pounds for charity until it was discontinued in 2016. Many of these events are still going strong today.

In addition to my interest in public transport, I also have an interest in the popular music of the late 1950s and early 1960s, in particular that of the eccentric independent record producer, songwriter and manager Joe Meek, in whose tiny studio above a shop in Holloway Road (not far from the famous trolleybus junction) he wrote and produced *Telstar* by The Tornados, which became the first British pop record to make No.1 in America, at the end of 1962, long before The Beatles had even been heard of over there! When Joe died in February 1967, I set up an Appreciation Society for his music, which has a very distinctive sound. That society is also still going strong today, too.

I also enjoy a pint or two (and usually more) of real ale, and I have two grown-up daughters, Margaret and Felicity, and four grandchildren, Gracie, Freddie, Oscar and Ava, at the time of writing. I still live in North London, having moved to my present home in Palmers Green in 1982.

INTRODUCTION

For many years, going back to the very first horse bus or tram operations in Victorian times, many towns and cities throughout Britain had their own operators, owned and run by the town or city councils. These were known as municipal operators. Most of them had had tramway systems, many of which were then replaced by trolleybuses from the 1920s onwards. Only those in Blackpool remained by the mid-1960s. In turn, after the Second World War, trolleybuses too were on the way out, with motorbuses unfortunately replacing both forms of electric traction. This book, however, illustrates only a few of these – the majority of my trolleybus pictures from this period are included in my other book *Trolleybus Twlilight* (Pen and Sword Transport, 2017).

At this period, some of these operators had very large fleets, for example those serving the conurbations of Birmingham, Liverpool and Manchester, whilst others had very small fleets, such as Bedwas & Machen Urban District Council in South Wales, and West Bridgford Urban District Council in Nottinghamshire.

Municipal operators had a wide variety of vehicle types, encompassing virtually all chassis and body makes then to be seen in service, and were also well known for their distinctive, traditional liveries. As the 1960s drew to a close, the fascinating array of vehicle types was rapidly being depleted as newer, standardised one man operated vehicles replaced the older ones, whilst also towards the end of the decade, government-inspired legislation forced the amalgamation of many of the smaller municipal operators into larger groupings, for example the South East Lancashire and Cheshire Passenger Transport Executive (SELNEC for short!) and the West Midlands PTE. Before long, the operators' distinctive liveries too became just a memory, therefore the period covered by this book illustrates the final chapter in the history of many British municipal operators in their original form.

Throughout most of the 1960s, I travelled to many of these operators and photographed their vehicles. I was fortunate to have been able to capture much of this changing transport scene on film and am pleased to be able to present some of my photographs in this volume. Most have never been published before.

I must put on record my thanks to the PSV Circle, from whose records most of the vehicle details included herein are taken, as well as to my old friends Paul Everett and Ken Wright, who were often with me when I took the photographs all those years ago and have helped refresh my memory regarding some of them. Also, may I thank Colin Clarke and John Scott-Morgan for helping make this book possible!

JIM BLAKE
Palmers Green
5 April 2015

Southend was one of the towns closest to London which had a municipal fleet. On 18 May 1964, their 1955 Leyland 'Titan' PD2/12 No.290 leaves their recently opened London Road depot. It has 55 seat lowbridge bodywork, built by Massey whose products often found favour with this operator.

A remarkable survivor seen inside the depot on the same occasion is 1931 AEC 'Regal' 5LW No.203. Its English Electric 30 seat bodywork has been extensively rebuilt by the Corporation, and by now it is used only on driver training duties.

Until 1954, Southend Corporation had operated trolleybuses. Somewhat ironically, some of the buses purchased to replace them were a batch of utility Daimler CWA6s acquired from London Transport and given new 55 seat Massey lowbridge bodies. Also on 18 May 1964, one of these, No.266, calls at Southend Victoria Station. This had been LT's D241, actually delivered in 1946. By now, they were being withdrawn.

Another seaside town not far from London to have its own municipal fleet was Brighton. This operator too had had trams and trolleybuses, the latter first appearing in 1939 and being withdrawn in the summer of 1961. Also dating from 1939, their Weymann-bodied AEC 'Regent' No.63 stands at Old Steine on 19 August 1964, by now used only on peak hour services. By chance, this vehicle has survived in preservation. Brighton Corporation shared its bus services with Tilling Group operator Brighton, Hove & District with both operators having a similar red and cream livery.

Further west along the South Coast, Portsmouth Corporation had a large fleet of buses. Unusual for a southern municipal operator, their No.50 is a Crossley DD42/7T with 58 seat Manchester style Crossley bodywork new in 1949. It is seen outside their Eastney depot, where traction standards for the city's trolleybuses, withdrawn a year previously, are still in place.

Another elderly Portsmouth Corporation double decker seen that day is No.181, a Weymann bodied Leyland 'Titan' PD1 dating from 1947. In this view, the trolleybus traction standards are used for street lighting and to display flower baskets!

Having started work for the London County Council in January 1965, I was now able to afford to travel further afield and made my first of many trips to the Midlands on 14 March 1965. This was to Leicester, whose Corporation's No.5, a 1948 AEC 'Regent' III with Birmingham style MCCW bodywork is seen here. A newer tin front Leyland PD3 stands behind.

Of similar vintage, No.62 is a Brush bodied AEC 'Regent' III. It is seen at the Corporation's Humberstone depot and is by now one of the last survivors of its batch.

Many municipal operators had by now acquired Leyland 'Atlanteans', but at this time, Leicester City Transport had only three early examples, of which 1960 built No.187 has MCCW 78 seat bodywork.

The operator closest to London which had trolleybuses was Maidstone Corporation. On 30 April 1965, in the town centre, Corporation trolleybus No.86 is a Weymann bodied Sunbeam W new in 1947, acquired from Maidstone & District when their Hastings and Bexhill trolleybus system closed in 1959.

I made the first of many trips to Birmingham on 4 July 1965, courtesy of a 'thirty bob' cheap day return from Paddington to Snow Hill. Outside the station, my first photograph of their huge fleet was of No. 1729, one of 100 Leyland 'Titan' PD2s with Brush 54 seat bodywork delivered in 1948. It is one of several of this batch based at Perry Barr garage.

Seen at Old Square amidst the drastic redevelopment works to Birmingham City Centre that were carried out in the mid-1960s, No.1890 is a 1948 Daimler CVG6 with very similar looking bodywork, albeit built by MCCW. This was because, as with London Transport, Birmingham had buses with different chassis and body makes designed to their own specification. This Daimler was one of nearly 400 delivered between 1948 and 1951 with MCCW bodywork, and was based at Lea Hall garage

Unusual in Birmingham's fleet in early post war years were a batch of fifty all Leyland 'Titan' PD2s built in 1949 which had standard Leyland 56-seat bodywork, rather than that built to the Corporation's specification. Of these, No.2156 works cross City route 90 near the Bull Ring.

Seen outside Birmingham's Selly Oak garage are MCCW 30 seat Leyland 'Tiger' PS2 No.2252, one of thirty supplied in 1950, and 1952 Guy 'Arab' IV No.2904. The latter is one of a batch of 100 supplied that year and typifies the Birmingham 'tin-front' style of the 1950s. It is also noteworthy that the entire registration range JOJ1 - 999 was used on the Corporation's buses, no doubt helped by the fact that they were also the licensing authority!

Back at Snow Hill, new office blocks rise in the background as West Bromwich No.191 works route 74 to Dudley, jointly operated with Birmingham City Transport. This is a Daimler CVG6, with Willowbrook 60 seat bodywork built in 1957.

I was so impressed by my visit to Birmingham City Transport that I went there again the following week, on 11 July 1965. Here at their Perry Barr garage is No.1620, a 1947 MCCW bodied Daimler CVG6 54-seater, now one of their oldest vehicles still in service.

Birmingham Corporation
No.2810 stands at the Suffolk Street terminus of route 22 in the city centre. It is one of 125 Daimler CVG6s built with MCCW bodies in 1952. Note the antiquated looking Corporation bus stop and timing clock on the right.

With Snow
Hill station as a backdrop, No.2660 has similar MCCW bodywork, but is a Daimler CVD6 dating from 1951. There were 150 buses in this batch.

Ipswich Corporation favoured AECs in the 1950s and 1960s. On 18 July 1965, their No.3 is seen in service on route 4. It is a Park Royal bodied AEC 'Regent' III new in 1950 and actually one of the first motor buses in the fleet, which had hitherto been entirely tram and then trolleybus!

Ipswich No.63 is an AEC 'Regent' V with Massey bodywork, new in 1964. It is seen at Priory Heath whilst taking a party of Omnibus Society members on a tour of the system.

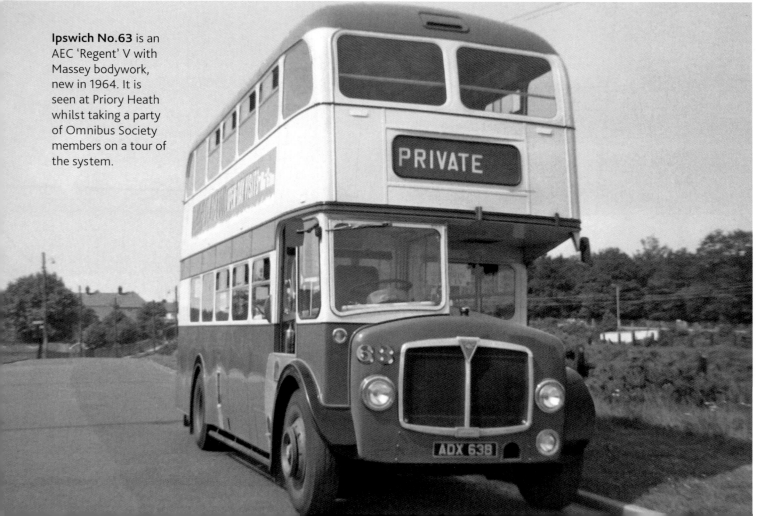

Seen outside Ipswich Corporation's Constantine Road depot is 1957 Park Royal bodied AEC 'Regent' V No.25. Note the destination 'Electric House', still the name of their headquarters despite trolleybus operation having ceased in 1963. The town's football ground is in the background.

Back in the town centre, No.12 works route 12 and is an AEC 'Regal' IV dating from 1952. Its Park Royal body is somewhat unusual in being of dual entrance configuration, seating 42.

At the same spot as No.3 seen earlier, No.21 is a Park Royal bodied AEC 'Regent' III, one of four built only in 1956 yet looking very similar to the original 1950 batch.

At Nottingham's Lower Parliament Street depot on 8 August 1965, No.311 is one of the Corporation's oldest buses still in service, a 1949 AEC 'Regent' III with unusual Roberts bodywork. It contrasts with two more recent Park Royal bodied 'Regents'.

No.203 is a lowbridge Park Royal bodied AEC 'Regent' III new in 1954 also seen at the depot. Will the trolleybus on the left ever run again? We will see some of these later.

The Urban District of West Bridgford, on the other side of the River Trent to the City of Nottingham, operated one of the smallest municipal fleets in the country, whose brown and cream buses contrasted with Nottingham's green and cream ones. Here at their depot is their No.27, a 1945 utility Daimler CWA6 with Duple 55 seat lowbridge utility bodywork. It has only just been withdrawn. By now, it was very rare for buses with their original wartime utility bodies to remain in service, since most were rebodied in the 1950s. This one had been new to Huddersfield Corporation and was acquired in 1955.

The following Sunday, 15 August 1965, I visited Coventry in whose Corporation's Hartnall Lane garage, No.24 is one of their last 1948 MCCW bodied 60 seat Daimler CVA6s still in service.

An oddity in the Coventry Corporation fleet is 1949 Daimler CVD6 No.113, one of two survivors with Brush dual purpose 30 seat bodywork. It stands at the entrance to Hartnall Lane garage.

A very unusual vehicle for a municipal fleet is Coventry No.504, a Bedford VAS2 with Marshall 30 seat bodywork, newly delivered when this picture was taken.

Odder still for a municipal fleet are these Walker bodied Commer 12 seat minibuses, which are also in Coventry's PSV fleet. Newly delivered, too, No.511 is nearest the camera, flanked by Nos 509 and 513.

The Sunday after that, 22 August 1965, I was back in Birmingham again! At the Corporation's Cotteridge depot, Crossley bodied Daimler CVG6 No.2847 is the only rear entrance double decker in the entire fleet to be fitted with platform doors.

It was as if I could not keep away from Birmingham in the summer of 1965, as I was there again on 29 August 1965! Here, 1950 all Crossley 55-seater No.2425 has literally been put out to grass with a number of other withdrawn Corporation vehicles outside Washwood Heath depot.

Two others awaiting the scrap dealer are 1947 MCCW bodied Daimler CVG6 54-seater No.1558 and 1949 similarly-bodied CVD6 No. 1987.

Also withdrawn owing to accident damage, and partly cannibalised for spares, is No.2227, the first of the batch of fifty Park Royal bodied Leyland 'Titan' PD2s built in 1949/1950 to be taken out of service by Birmingham City Transport.

Still very much in
the land of the living
is Birmingham's
No.2747, a Daimler
CVD6 with MCCW
54 seat bodywork
new in 1951. It is seen
amid redevelopment
works at Old Square,
working route 14
from Lea Hall garage.

A visit to Southend
Corporation's
London Road depot
on the next day,
August Bank Holiday
Monday 30 August
1965, finds their
No.260, a Massey
bodied lowbridge
AEC 'Regent' III
dating from 1950,
and now one of
the oldest buses in
the fleet.

Amid Bank Holiday crowds at Pier Hill, Southend 1956 'tin-front' Leyland 'Titan' PD2/20 No.299 carries Weymann 58 seat lowbridge bodywork, needed to enable it to pass beneath the approaches to the famous pier, which it is just about to do. On the right at the top of this picture, one of Eastern National's Bristol FLF 'Lodekka' coaches used on express service X10 may also be seen. The surroundings here have changed completely in the fifty years since I took this photograph.

The second municipal bus operator in Essex was Colchester Corporation. On 7 September 1965, their No.54 is a 1947 Massey bodied 56 seat highbridge AEC 'Regent' II, now due for early withdrawal when seen at the town's bus station.

Another elderly double decker in Colchester's fleet is Roberts bodied Daimler CVD6 No.1, built in 1949. It arrives at the bus station in this view.

A visit to Southampton on 19 September 1965 finds their No.306, a Leyland 'Titan' PD2/27 new in 1960 with rather ungainly looking Park Royal 66 seat bodywork, seen at Portswood.

Seen at Southampton Docks, 1963 AEC 'Regent' V No.353 has much nicer looking Neepsend bodywork and also seats 66.

Eastbourne was another South Coast seaside town whose Corporation ran the town's local services. An Omnibus Society visit to their depot on 26 September 1965 sees the pride of their fleet driven out for photographs outside their depot. This is No.12, a 1939 Leyland 'Lion' LT9 still with its original Leyland 32 seat body and used for school and private hire work.

Crossley No.2155 is a DD42/7 dating from 1948 and has recently been withdrawn. It too has Crossley bodywork of the standard Manchester style of the period.

A small number of Manchester trolleybuses remained in service at this period, all being BUT 9612Ts with Burlingham 70 seat bodywork dating from 1955. This is No.1362, working route 216 to Stalybridge where Manchester trolleybuses shared the wires with Ashton-Under-Lyne ones.

An older Manchester motor bus still in service is 1948 Leyland 'Titan' PD1/3 No.3111, one of 200 of this type bodied by MCCW for the Corporation in 1947/1948. It is seen under the wires working limited stop route 24 to Rochdale.

Oldham was yet another town in the area to have its own corporation buses, which served Manchester too. Here at the terminus of their route 24 in Manchester, the driver of their 1964 Roe bodied Leyland 'Titan' PD3/5 73-seater No.104 looks somewhat puzzled as a friend of mine, seen bending over on the right, scrapes its nearside dumbiron to ascertain its Leyland chassis frame number! These apparently differed from their actual chassis numbers and he had exhaustive records of them throughout the country.

More typical of Oldham's fleet at the time is their No.350, a Roe bodied Leyland 'Titan' PD2/3 56-seater new in 1948. Livery of this fleet was maroon and white.

We travelled to Oldham that day, and here in their depot yard are a group of 1946 Roe bodied Leyland 'Titan' PD1s. They have recently been ordered off the road by the Transport Commissioner as being unfit for service, and the three nearest the camera, Nos 234, 228 and 238 have notices in their windscreens to prove it!

A look inside Oldham's depot shows that Roe bodied 1948 Leyland 'Titan' PD2/3 No.347 has lost its roof. Next to it, No.407, a 'tin front' 'Titan' PD2/20 built in 1957, also with Roe bodywork, has not been overhauled since it was new, and therefore is also off the road!

Such were the problems with Oldham Corporation's buses at this time that second-hand vehicles from other operators had to be purchased to keep services going. Their No.466 is an all Leyland 'Titan' PD2/1 dating from 1948 and recently acquired from Sheffield Corporation.

A real oddity in Oldham's depot is No.324, one of fifteen Daimler CVD6s with Manchester style Crossley 56 seat bodies, new to the Corporation in 1949.

Another real oddity tucked away in Oldham's depot is No.299, a Crossley SD42/3 built in 1948, originally with a Roe 32 seat body and one of a batch of ten. However, this was in such poor condition by 1965, that the body was scrapped and replaced by a 'new' Crossley 32 seat body that had originally been new to Southport Corporation No.117, a Crossley SD42/7 new in 1951!

Oldham No.364 is a Crossley SD42/7, with Roe 32 seat bodywork new in 1951 and one of two survivors of an original batch of four. It looks in somewhat shaky condition, however, as well as appearing much older than it really is!

An unusual single decker of an entirely different kind seen in Oldham's depot that day is school bus 203FBU, a 40 seat Seddon 'Pennine' built in 1963.

A vehicle whose services Oldham Corporation must have needed at this period is their breakdown tender, which is a pre-war all Leyland 'Titan' TD4 once numbered 209 in their bus fleet!

Still going strong, however, is Oldham No.284, a Leyland 'Titan' PD1/3 with Roe 56 seat bodywork, one of fifty delivered in 1947/1948 and seen on one of the town's local services.

We also visited Ashton-Under-Lyne that day. Their oldest bus is No.1, an all Leyland 'Titan' PD2/3 dating from 1950 seen in the town's bus station.

At the bus station too is No.38, a Guy 'Arab' IV with rare Bond 60 seat bodywork, one of four new in 1956.

Inside Ashton's depot, 1963 Roe bodied Leyland 'Titan' PD2/40 No.36 contrasts with 1945 Guy 'Arab' II No.72. This also has a Roe body, seating 56 and fitted in 1955 to replace its original wartime utility bodywork.

Ashton No.28 is another Leyland 'Titan' PD2/40 with Roe 65 seat bodywork, this time dating from 1961. This operator's smartly turned out buses are a marked contrast to those seen in Oldham earlier!

Another municipal operator to serve Ashton-Under-Lyne was the curiously named Stalybridge, Hyde, Mossley and Dunkinfield Transport & Electricity Board (usually referred to as SHMD for short!). Looking smart in their green and cream livery is their No.86, a 64 seat Northern Counties bodied Leyland 'Titan' PD2/40 new in 1958.

Also seen in Ashton, SHMD No.105 is a unique Daimler 'Freeline' G6H single decker built in 1953 with Northern Counties 34 seat dual entrance bodywork, plus space for 27 standees.

Another unusual SHMD single decker with Northern Counties dual entrance 34 seat plus 27 standee bodywork is No.109, a rare Atkinson PL745H, one of two new in 1956.

Seen on the same day in Salford Bus Station, Salford City Transport No.414 is another Daimler, a CVG6D with MCCW bodywork dating from 1950. It is now one of the oldest buses in their fleet, and due for early withdrawal.

Back in Manchester proper, 1955 Burlingham bodied BUT trolleybus No.1302 contrasts with North Western 1949 Weymann bodied Leyland 'Titan' PD2/1 No. 252.

A municipal operator not seen so often in Manchester is Rawtenstall Corporation, whose 1958 East Lancs 43 seat Leyland 'Tiger Cub' PSUC1/1 No.58 is seen at Lower Mosley Street Bus Station.

The Cheshire
town of Stockport,
to the south of
Manchester, also had
its own municipal
fleet; somewhat
confusingly, their
buses were in a red
and white livery
rather similar to
that of BET fleet
North Western,
who had their
headquarters there.
Here on 6 August
1966, Stockport
Corporation 1948 all
Leyland 'Titan' PD2/1
56-seater No.273
is seen at Mersey
Square Bus Station.

A real rarity for this
area is Stockport's
No.350, a Leyland
'Titan' PD2/30
which is one of ten
supplied in 1960 with
61 seat Longwell
Green bodywork.
This Bristol based
manufacturer rarely
produced bodies for
fleets beyond the
South Wales or West
Country area.

Another oddity in the Stockport fleet is No.340, also a Leyland 'Titan' PD2/30, but this time with Crossley 61 seat bodywork built in 1958. Its batch of ten were the last Crossley bodied buses to be produced. The vehicle stands beneath the viaduct carrying the main line from Manchester Piccadilly to Crewe and the south.

Changing crew outside Stockport Corporation's Mersey Square depot is 1951 all Leyland 'Titan' PD2/1 56-seater No.288. On the extreme right, tram tracks may just be discerned leading into the depot. Trams were abandoned here in 1950.

In the depot, No.327 is one of twenty-four Crossley DD42/7s built in 1951 with Crossley 56 seat bodywork. Stockport was this manufacturer's hometown.

Inside the Corporation's other depot at Heaton Lane is Stockport Welfare Department's JA7585, a 1938 Leyland 'Tiger' TS8 still with its original pre-war English Electric 34 seat centre entrance bodywork. It was withdrawn from the public bus fleet in 1963.

We travelled on to Hyde that day, where we discovered another pre-war survivor. This is SHMD 1939 Northern Counties bodied Daimler COG5 FTU132 in use as a staff canteen at the town's bus station.

One of the oldest buses still in service with SHMD is No.47, a 1949 Daimler CVD6 with East Lancs 56 seat bodywork. It is in Hyde Bus Station bound for Stockport, Edgeley.

Stabled for the night at SHMD's Park Road, Stalybridge depot No.72 and two of its fellows are part of a batch of six Daimler CVG6s built in 1956 with very unusual Northern Counties 58 seat centre entrance bodywork.

Another very unusual Daimler stabled at this depot is SHMD No.101, a Daimler CVG5 with single deck Northern Counties 35 seat bodywork. The other four buses of this batch, dating from 1950, were CVD6s.

One of Rotherham's last Bristol double deckers is 1950 East Lancs bodied KS6B highbridge 56-seater No.108. Very few Bristol KSs were built with bodies other than those produced by ECW.

Another unusual vehicle in the Rotherham fleet is No.210, one of six highbridge 56 seat Crossley bodied DD42/8s new in 1952. Livery is royal blue and cream.

As well as Crossleys, Rotherham purchased Daimlers after their supply of Bristol buses was denied. No.228 is a CVG6 with Weymann 56 seat bodywork new in 1954.

A more modern Rotherham single decker seen on this occasion is 1959 AEC 'Reliance' No.167, which carries a Weymann 45 seat body.

Rotherham turned to AEC for their double deckers in later years, too. No.140 is an AEC 'Bridgemaster' with ungainly looking Park Royal 70 seat bodywork, new in 1961.

A seaside holiday at Hastings in the last two weeks of August 1966 enabled me to visit Brighton, Eastbourne and Maidstone again. At Brighton's Old Steine on 22 August 1966 is Brighton Corporation's No.84, a 1947 AEC 'Regent' III with Weymann 56 seat bodywork. This batch of buses was due for withdrawal after the 1966 summer season.

Of similar appearance and manufacture, but seating 58, Weymann bodied AEC 'Regent' III No.91 dates from 1950. It accompanies a Brighton, Hove & District Bristol 'Lodekka' outside Brighton Station.

A newer Brighton Corporation double decker seen at Old Steine is No.54, a Leyland 'Titan' PD2/37 with Weymann 'Orion' 61 seat bodywork built for trolleybus replacement in 1959. Two Brighton, Hove & District Bristol 'Lodekkas' working joint services with the Corporation stand behind it, the white one, somewhat oddly, is a convertible open topper with its roof on on this sunny August day!

Next day, 23 August 1966, I visited Maidstone. Their 56 seat 1946 Northern Counties bodied Sunbeam W trolleybus No.65 is one of just two of its type still operating when seen bound for Loose. It is in the Corporation's smart light brown and cream livery.

Somewhat oddly, Maidstone Corporation's trolleybuses were worked on the same routes as the buses that replaced them during their last months of operation. One of their replacements, 1965 Leyland 'Atlantean' No.32, which has an unusual Massey 75 seat body and sports the Corporation's new blue and cream livery, is seen at Barming, Bull Inn terminus.

On 24 August 1966, I travelled along the coast to Eastbourne, where the Corporation's 1948 East Lancs/ Bruce bodied 56 seat Leyland 'Titan' PD2/1 No.26 is seen at the terminus of their route 2. This Titan is due for early withdrawal.

Replacements for elderly Leyland 'Titan' PD2s like the one seen above were also Leyland 'Titan' PD2s! Brand new PD2A/30 No.79 also has East Lancs bodywork, seating 60, and looks immaculate in the Corporation's dark blue and cream livery when seen in the town centre. However, in the intervening years between these two buses being built, Eastbourne also bought a number of AEC 'Regent' Vs.

I was back in Liverpool again on 4 September 1966, visiting a number of the Corporation's depots. Here at Green Lane depot, D600 is the last Daimler in the Corporation's fleet, a CVD6 built in 1947 with Weymann 56 seat bodywork. It now, however, awaits disposal.

Also awaiting disposal at Green Lane, 1948 Weymann 56 seat AEC 'Regent' III A547 has suffered serious accident damage to its nearside lower deck. This was one of more than 200 'Regent' IIIs with Weymann body frames which were completed in Liverpool's own workshops.

A Leyland awaiting disposal also at Green Lane is L419, a 1952 'Titan' PD2/12, with Weymann 56 seat bodywork.

Liverpool L10 is another Weymann bodied Leyland 'Titan' PD2/12, built in 1953, seen standing in the sun at the entrance to Litherland depot.

An older Leyland 'Titan' PD2/1, this time with Leyland 56 seat bodywork dating from 1948, is L446, one of many based at the Corporation's Stanley depot and seen in its yard, which is actually opposite the Green Lane depot where the withdrawn vehicles above were stored!

Out in service, and well laden on that Sunday, Liverpool 1958 Crossley bodied Leyland 'Titan' PD2/20 62-seater L367 passes the Corporation's bus repair and overhaul works in Carnegie Road, bound for Aigburth.

Nearer to my north London home, Southend Corporation open topper No.246 is seen on the seafront of its hometown beneath the lights for the illuminations on 17 September 1966. This is a wartime Daimler CWA6 new in 1944, whose Duple utility body was heavily rebuilt when converted to open top. It was acquired from Eastern National in 1955 and by now was the only one of its batch still in service.

One of Southend's newest buses at this period is No.336, a Massey 70 seat bodied Leyland 'Titan' PD3/6 new in 1965 but looking much older than that. Though with standard transverse upper deck seating, these buses had special low height bodies to enable them to pass beneath the pier approach. During 1975/1976, these buses were loaned to London Transport and London Country to cover for a shortage of 'Routemasters'. Ironically, in the late 1980s and early 1990s, the route this bus is working, the 29, was operated by ex-London 'Routemasters' bought by Southend Transport!

Wolverhampton Corporation still operated trolleybuses at this period, and a trip to the city on 25/9/66 finds their No.432, one of the oldest still in service, working route 58 from Wolverhampton to Dudley via Sedgley. Its badly bent booms illustrate how the system is being run down. This trolleybus is a Sunbeam W new in 1945, whose original utility body was replaced by a new Roe one, seating 60, in 1958. Livery is green and cream.

In order to assist with trolleybus replacement, a number of Birmingham City Transport Daimlers were sold to Wolverhampton Corporation in 1964. 1949 MCCW 54 seat CVD6 No.2002 is one of two seen at Fallings Park depot.

A badly accident-damaged Wolverhampton vehicle at Fallings Park is 1963 Park Royal bodied dual entrance 40 seat AEC 'Reliance' No.705, which will no doubt be repaired. Abandoned trolleybus overhead hangs above it!

Wolverhampton Corporation also had their own Daimlers. This is No.523, a CVG6 built in 1949 with Brush 54 seat bodywork.

It was only natural that Wolverhampton would have a large number of Guy buses, considering that this manufacturer was based in the city. No.551 is a Guy 'Arab' III built in 1950. Its Park Royal 54 seat body has had the front of its upper deck rebuilt, resulting in this rather odd appearance.

One of the last Guy 'Arabs' in the fleet is No.167, an 'Arab' V with MCCW 72 seat forward entrance bodywork delivered in 1965.

Somewhat oddly, however, Wolverhampton Corporation only bought two of Guy's ill fated 'Wulfrunians'. The first, No.70 which was delivered in 1961 with East Lancs 72 seat bodywork, is seen out of use at Fallings Park depot. The odd position of the staircase, to the front nearside of the vehicle, may just be discerned.

The second 'Wulfrunian', No.71 built in 1962 also with East Lancs bodywork but seating 71, is still in service when seen also at Fallings Park depot on 25 September 1966. It has its staircase in the conventional position for a front entrance double decker, on the offside.

Following the cessation of bus chassis production by Guy, Wolverhampton Corporation turned to AEC. No.182 is a newly delivered 'Renown' with 70 seat Park Royal forward entrance bodywork. Its crew stand beside it and it is noteworthy that the conductor is a Sikh, wearing his turban. There was at this period much argument as to whether bus crews should be allowed to wear such obligatory religious headgear, especially in this area where the local MP Enoch Powell made his 'Rivers of Blood' speech some eighteen months after this picture was taken, alluding to the large numbers of immigrants coming to Britain from the Indian sub-continent, the West Indies and Africa. Happily, eventually operators allowed staff to wear turbans – where would they have been without staff recruited from overseas?

A surprising vehicle still in service with Preston Corporation on 8 October 1966 is No.74, a 1949 Leyland 'Tiger' PS1/1 with East Lancs 34 seat rear entrance bodywork.

I had stopped briefly in Preston on the way to visit Blackpool for the weekend. In their depot, traditional 'standard' tramcar No.147 is one of four survivors of a batch built by the Corporation in the mid-1920s with Dick Kerr four wheel trucks and BTH motors. It seated 78. A number of the Corporation's famous 'balloon cars' accompany it, along with one of the special cars used during the illuminations.

One of the 'balloon cars', No.259, is about to pass Blackpool Tower beneath the illuminations on its way to the Pleasure Beach. There were twenty-seven of these trams, which were centre entrance 84 or 94-seaters built by English Electric in 1934/1935. At busy times, they had a conductor on each deck. All were still in service in 1966; a few survive in Blackpool today, more than eighty years after they were built!

At this period, single deck tram No.224 was one of only two examples of this type of English Electric 48-seater still in service. They were built in 1934. As may be seen, its bodywork closely resembles the lower deck of the 'balloon cars' built by the same manufacturer.

Blackpool had more modern single deck trams, too. No.312 seen heading for Fleetwood is one of twenty-five built by Charles Roberts between 1952 and 1954, with Maley and Taunton 4 wheel truck and Crompton Parkinson motors.

My reason for visiting Manchester on that cold, gloomy December Saturday was to attend a tour organised by the PSV Circle marking the withdrawal of Manchester Corporation's last Crossleys. One of two used, No.2139, a DD42/7 with Crossley 58 seat bodywork, is seen under the wires in the Hyde Road disposal yard.

Awaiting disposal is No.2068, an earlier Crossley DD42/4 58-seater new in 1948. Manchester City Transport had nearly 300 similar vehicles, built between 1946 and 1949.

A really antique vehicle at Hyde Road is VR5742, a Leyland 'Lion' dating from 1929 which had been in use for many years as a staff canteen. Like the Nottingham single decker seen earlier, it too has a water tank on its roof.

By 15 January 1967, the Bournemouth trolleybus system was also in terminal decline. Here at the Corporation's Mallard Road depot, Nos 259 and 261 are amongst a group of Weymann bodied 'Sunbeam' MF2Bs built only in 1958 that will never run again.

Inside the depot are two Bournemouth Corporation Daimler 'Fleetlines'. 1965 Alexander bodied No.195 is one of several of this type in the fleet with Weymann 74 seat bodywork, but No.40 is a real oddity. It is one of two built in 1964 with MH Coachworks (Belfast) 74 seat bodies, originally meant for use in Northern Ireland.

One of several single deckers in the Bournemouth fleet, No.99 is a Park Royal bodied Leyland 'Tiger Cub' PSUC1/1 42-seater new in 1955, seen under the wires in the town centre.

Sunday, 5 March 1967 was the last day of trolleybus operation in Wolverhampton. Here, their 1947 'Sunbeam' W No.444 passes the city's ABC Cinema on route 58 bound for Dudley. These trolleybuses were given new Roe 60 seat bodies built only between 1958 and 1962 – what a waste!

At Wolverhampton's Cleveland Road depot, CET440 is a former Rotherham Corporation Bristol L5G single decker built in 1940, whose East Lancs body was adapted for use as a tower wagon and towing vehicle. It has actually towed a preserved Rotherham trolleybus here to run on the last day of Wolverhampton's trolleybuses!

One of the oldest double deckers still in service in Wolverhampton Corporation's motorbus fleet is No.534, a Daimler CVG6 with Brush 54 seat bodywork new in 1950. These formed a small minority, the vast majority being locally built 'Guys'.

Of the same vintage, withdrawn Guy 'Arab' III single decker No.563 has been fitted as a snowplough, yet still carries route and number blinds! It has Guy 34 seat rear entrance bodywork and is one of two survivors built in 1949 retained for this purpose.

As mentioned above, most of Wolverhampton Corporation's double deckers were Guys, built as late as 1966 at their Falling's Park factory which was close to the Corporation's depot in that suburb. No.19 was a unique vehicle in their fleet, a Guy 'Arab' IV built in 1958 with Burlingham full fronted 68 seat bodywork. A large batch of 'Arab' IVs with MCCW bodywork of similar style followed between 1959 and 1961.

Two conventional Guy 'Arab' IVs seen in the depot are No.16, with MCCW 60 seat bodywork new in 1957 and No.577, built in 1953 with a Roe 56 seat body. Both have typical 'tin-front' radiator grilles of their period. Behind them, on the left, is No.28, one of the full front MCCW bodied 'Arab' IVs built in 1959 and seating 72.

An Omnibus Touring Circle visit to Coventry on 19 March 1967 finds the Corporation's 1962 MCCW 'Orion' bodied Daimler CVG6 63-seater No.306 setting off from Pool Meadow bus station.

At the Corporation's Harnall Lane East depot, No.96 is one of a group of Daimler CVA6s demoted to training duties. It carries Birmingham style MCCW 60 seat bodywork and dates from 1952, delivered for some reason much later than others in its batch.

A more recent Coventry Daimler seen at the depot is No.138, an MCCW bodied 58 seat CVD6 new in 1951.

A gloomy, wet Sunday 2 April 1967 finds Derby Corporation 1966 Roe bodied Daimler 'Fleetline' No.182 working route 51A, which was jointly operated with BET fleet Trent Motor Traction.

A trip to South Wales on 8 April 1967 took me to Newport, where the Corporation's 1950 Leyland 'Titan' PD2/3 No.31 is seen passing the Western Region station. In common with many of this fleet's buses it has unusual bodywork, in this case built by Bruce Coachworks on East Lancs frames and seating 56.

Even odder is Newport Corporation's No.49, which is a Dennis 'Lancet' UF built in 1956 with D.J. Davies of Tredegar bodywork on Park Royal frames, seating 42 with a rear entrance! It is seen at Newport's Corporation Road depot. There were eight of these peculiar vehicles, together with another four similar ones with standard front entrance bodywork.

Newport No.41 is one of the four front entrance 'Lancets' mentioned above, built in 1954 and seating 44. The rear entrance of another of the eight so fitted is visible in front of it. A Longwell Green bodied Leyland 'Titan' PD2/40 brings up the rear. They are seen in Newport Bus Station.

A more straightforward Newport Corporation vehicle is No.26, last of twenty Guy 'Arab' IIIs built in 1949/1950 with Guy 56 seat bodies constructed on Park Royal frames. It is also seen at the town's bus station.

My next port of call that day was Cardiff, at whose Newport Road depot, trolleybus No.211 is about to take up service. This is the first of a batch of twenty BUT 9641Ts new in 1948 with East Lancs 67 seat dual entrance/exit bodywork. A withdrawn Bruce bodied AEC 'Regent' III awaits disposal on the right.

At Cardiff Corporation's Sloper Road depot is No.6, a Bruce bodied AEC 'Regent' III 59-seater built in 1950 and now one of their oldest motor buses in service. Behind it is an East Lancs bodied Daimler CVG6.

Another elderly 'Regent' III at Sloper Road is No.18, also dating from 1950 but with East Lancs 59 seat bodywork. The other buses in this view illustrate what a varied fleet Cardiff Corporation had at the time.

An even older double decker at the depot is No.93, a 1946 Bristol K6A with heavily rebuilt Duple utility 56 seat bodywork. It is now demoted to training duties.

The next operator to lose trolleybuses was Maidstone Corporation, just six weeks after Wolverhampton! On their last day of service, 15 April 1967, No.58 is a wartime Sunbeam, originally bodied by Park Royal in 1944 and given a new Roe body only in 1960. It is bound for Barming.

Replacements for Maidstone's last trolleybuses were Massey bodied Leyland 'Atlanteans', which ran alongside them in their final weeks. Brand new No.42 is seen under the wires in the town centre, showing off the Corporation's new light blue and cream livery.

Also under the wires, Maidstone Corporation Leyland 'Titan' PD2 No.21 also has Massey bodywork, still bearing their earlier orange/brown and cream livery. Buses of both this type and the newer 'Atlanteans' were loaned to London Country to help with vehicle shortages some nine or ten years later.

At Southampton on 23 April 1967, brand new East Lancs 70 seat AEC 'Regent' V No.392 is the last of twenty of this type recently delivered to the Corporation fleet.

Southampton Corporation had nearly 200 Park Royal bodied Guy 'Arab' III 56-seaters delivered in the early post-war years. One of the last was No.66, part of a batch of ten delivered in 1954, seen here arriving at Shirley depot. The Timpson's Harrington bodied coach on the right has taken me there on an Omnibus Touring Circle visit.

At the Corporation's other depot at Portswood is No.258, an Alexander 31 seat Albion 'Nimbus' MR9N, one of three delivered in 1956/1957, and quite rare for an English municipal operator.

The only other single deckers in Southampton's fleet at this time were four Park Royal bodied Guy 'Arab' UF 39-seaters delivered in 1954. Of these, No.252 is also seen at Portswood.

Withdrawal of Southampton's earlier Guy 'Arabs' was now progressing. No.179 and No.180 of the 1949 batch await disposal at Portswood.

As often with coastal operators, Southampton cut down some of its older double deckers for seafront service. No.33 is one of two Park Royal bodied Guy 'Arab' IIs delivered in 1946 so treated and painted in cream livery, as opposed to the Corporation's usual maroon and cream.

Thanks to further extension northwards of the M1 motorway, we were able to reach Sheffield on the OTC's May 1967 trip! On 21 May 1967, Sheffield Corporation No.1009 is seen in the city centre and is a Burlingham bodied Leyland 'Leopard' new in 1960.

In complete contrast to the half-cab Leylands and Guys seen above, is this 1964 Birkenhead Corporation Daimler 'Fleetline' with MCCW bodywork, seen at New Ferry terminus.

Despite trying rear engined Daimler 'Fleetlines' in 1964, Birkenhead Corporation reverted to their tried and trusted combination of Leyland 'Titan' chassis and Massey rear entrance bodywork in 1965. One of these, No.113, is also at New Ferry. Birkenhead's light blue and cream livery suits it well.

A similar combination of chassis and body was delivered in 1967, too, being some of the last Leyland 'Titan' PD3s ever built. Brand new No.144 has just arrived at New Ferry amid an array of other Birkenhead vehicles.

A second municipal operator on the Wirral peninsular was Wallasey Corporation, whose buses were in a livery described as sea green and cream. This is their No.41, a Leyland 'Titan' PD2/1 with rather antique looking MCCW 56 seat bodywork new in 1951.

A very strange vehicle seen at Wallasey Corporation's Seaview Road depot also on 1 July 1967 is No.81, which has a Leyland 'Titan' PD2/10 chassis new in 1957 and usually bodied as a double decker and a 1948 Burlingham 29 seat coach body, which had originally been fitted to a pre-war chassis! It had in fact been withdrawn in 1965 but remained out of use, though intact, in the depot yard.

Another oddity, delivered at the same time and consecutively registered is Wallasey No.43, also a 1957 'Titan' PD2/10, but carrying the 1951 MCCW 56 seat body new to the original No.43, whose chassis was destroyed in an accident in 1959. This begs the question as to where this chassis was in 1957/1958? Next to it, No.74 is less exotic, being one of ten PD2/12 'Titans' delivered in 1952 with Weymann 56 seat bodies.

Wallasey Corporation was the first British operator to place a production Leyland 'Atlantean' in service, in 1958. This is their No.2, first of the 1959 batch, bearing a MCCW 77 seat body and one of a batch of thirty built between 1958 and 1961. It stands outside Seaview Road depot.

Another unusual single decker in the Wallasey fleet is No.33, one of four Albion 'Nimbuses' with Strachans 31 seat dual purpose bodywork built in 1962.

Wallasey No.64 is one of a dozen Leyland 'Titan' PD2/12s with Weymann 56 seat bodies new in 1951 and is seen at New Ferry terminus on route 10, jointly worked with Birkenhead Corporation. Both operators were swallowed up within Merseyside PTE in 1969.

With Cammell Laird's famous Birkenhead shipyard behind them, Birkenhead Corporation No.371 is one of five Leyland 'Titan' PD2/12s with Weymann 'Orion' 59 seat bodies new in 1955, whereas No.270 is one of five PD2/12s built in 1954 with rare Ashcroft 59 seat bodies.

Having taken the ferry across the Mersey, I am now in Liverpool where 1954 Crossley/LCPT 56 seat AEC 'Regent' III A46 displays blinds for Penny Lane, after which the Beatles named one of their hit records. Earlier 'Regent' III A733, built in 1951 with a Weymann framed 56 seat body completed locally, accompanies it.

At Derby's Market Place terminus on 2 July 1967, we see the Corporation's Roe bodied Sunbeam F4A trolleybus No.239, a 65-seater built only in 1960. Sadly, this system will be abandoned two months later.

Despite being considerably older than the trolleybuses, 1950 56 seat Brush bodied Daimler CVD6 No.91 will survive them! It too is seen under the wires arriving at Derby's Market Place.

A visit to Lincoln City Transport's St. Mark's depot on a dismal 13 August 1967 finds their No.23, a 1948 Guy bodied Guy 'Arab' III 56-seater modified to operate with an air-cooled Ruston & Hornsby diesel engine, hence the unusual radiator grille!

Working the same route, No.33 is a Roe bodied AEC 'Reliance', one of three built in 1960, seating 41 and also with dual entrance/exit layout.

Also an AEC 'Reliance', No.42 is one of four dual entrance 41-seaters with Willowbrook bodies, supplied in 1962.

No.207 represents the older generation of Sunderland's double deckers and is seen in murky conditions near the docks. It is one of the second batch of a dozen Daimler CVG5s built in 1954 with Roe 63 seat bodies, which helped complete replacement of the Corporation's trams in that year.

Nearest the camera in this line-up of buses outside Sunderland Corporation's Fulwell depot, Nos 180, 177 and 179 are part of a batch of two dozen Guy 'Arab' IVs built in 1954, unusually with Crossley 63 seat bodywork. They look smart in their dark green and cream livery.

Odd man out in the line-up of buses seen above, No.145 is an exposed radiator Daimler CVG5 with Roe 58 seat bodywork new in 1953, one of a batch of eight.

Now relegated to training duties and renumbered 238, this Guy 'Arab' II was new in 1943 with a wartime utility body, but rebodied by Roe with this 61 seat body in 1954 and was originally No.67 in the Corporation's operational fleet.

Passing near the depot. No.159 is one of the first batch of twenty Roe bodied Daimler CVG5 63-seaters built in 1954.

In complete contrast to the 1950s double deckers seen above, Sunderland No.80 is a high capacity Leyland 'Panther' with Strachans bodywork new in 1966. It is seen here loading up in the town centre outside Binns, the department store which was advertised on the front of so many double deck buses in this area.

Sadly, I only paused in the City of Newcastle briefly, when changing trains to return from Sunderland to Carlisle, and have not been there before or since! Fortunately, I was able to photograph a couple of the Corporation's strikingly liveried yellow and cream buses, and this one, No.351 is one of just three Leyland 'Titan' PD2/20s with MCCW 'Orion' 60 seat bodies new in 1954. And after very murky weather across the River Tyne in Sunderland, the sun has come out for the evening!

Also outside Newcastle Central Station, at the terminus of route 7 to Throckley, No.186 is one of ten Leyland 'Titan' PD3/1s with MCCW 'Orion' 72 seat bodies built in 1957. Newcastle's bus fleet at this time was composed almost entirely of AECs and Leylands.

I visited the city of Chester on the last day of my railrover, 1 September 1967, and, sadly, the weather was poor then too! In the gloom outside the corporation's Station Street depot, No.19 is a Massey bodied Guy 'Arab' IV 60-seater, one of five new in 1957. Tram tracks are still discernible in the cobbles, 37 years after the Chester trams' demise!

Also with Massey bodywork, Chester Corporation No.78 is a rare Foden PVD6 56-seater, built in 1950. Eight of these were supplied to the fleet between 1948 and 1951. It is seen outside Chester General Station, and it has now begun to rain!

Massey bodywork was favoured by Chester Corporation for many years and is also on No.10, a 56 seat Guy 'Arab' IV built in 1954. It collects rain-sodden passengers near the station.

A remarkable vehicle to be in the Chester fleet is No.51, a 1951 AEC 'Regal' III with East Lancs 35 seat rear entrance bodywork acquired from Nottingham Corporation in 1963. It is seen outside the historic King's Head hotel, which is reputed to be haunted, in the city centre.

Passing another historic and reputedly haunted Chester hotel, the Royal Oak, No.16 is one of six Massey bodied Guy 'Arab' IV 58-seaters new in 1958.

Amid a procession of Chester Corporation buses in historic Northgate Street, No.1, on route 1, is one of three 56 seat Massey bodied exposed radiator Guy 'Arab' IVs new in 1953.

Although looking like a Park Royal body, that mounted onto No.4 (one of four Guy 'Arab' IVs new in 1954) was actually built by Guy on Park Royal frames. It too is seen in Northgate Street.

A more modern Guy in Chester's fleet is No.29, an 'Arab' IV built in 1962 with Massey 73 seat forward entrance bodywork. Its bonnet and radiator grille are of a type originally produced by this manufacturer for Johannesburg in South Africa.

No.34 is one of four Guy 'Arab' Vs with Massey 73 seat forward entrance bodywork built in 1963 and is rather carelessly parked at the city centre terminus of route 1.

Back in Northgate Street, No.52 is a Leyland 'Leopard' single decker with Massey bodywork new in 1966.

Delivered at the same time, No.40 has the latest style of Massey forward entrance 73 seat bodywork on a Guy 'Arab' V chassis. Chester's brown and cream livery suits it.

In complete contrast, No.56 is one of two Guy 'Arab' IIs with Park Royal 56 seat bodywork new in 1946 to Southampton Corporation and acquired by Chester in 1959. It passes beneath Northgate with a Massey bodied 'Arab' III following as the weather gets even worse! After this, I returned home!

Here is another Massey bodied brown and cream Corporation double decker in equally appalling weather! Most ironically, two days later, on Sunday 3 September 1967, an enthusiasts' trip to Colchester Corporation was 'blessed' by atrocious weather too! Their No.10, one of three 56 seat AEC 'Regent' IIIs new in 1953, changes crew outside their Magdalen Street depot.

The pouring rain gives a somewhat 'atmospheric' quality to this view of No.55 leaving the depot! It is a solitary Crossley DD42/3 with Massey 56 seat bodywork new in 1948.

In the dry inside the depot is No.21, one of three Massey bodied AEC 'Regent' V 61-seaters new in 1959.

Illustrating more recent styles of Colchester Corporation livery, No. 24 and No. 26 are Massey 61 seat Leyland 'Titan' PD2/31s new in 1960, contrasting with 1959 'Regent' V No.23.

Back outside braving the elements, No.13 is a Massey 61 seat AEC 'Regent' V new in 1956 still bearing Colchester's earlier livery.

Warrington Corporation No.108 is a very unusual Foden PVD6 with East Lancs 58 seat bodywork and one of five built in 1956. It is seen on 9 September 1967 in the town's bus station, in the company of an equally unusual North Western Strachans bodied Bedford 'VAL'!

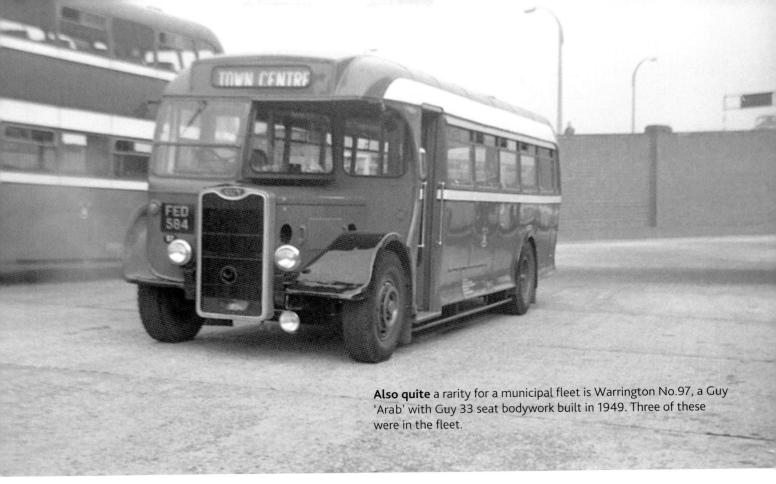

Also quite a rarity for a municipal fleet is Warrington No.97, a Guy 'Arab' with Guy 33 seat bodywork built in 1949. Three of these were in the fleet.

At Widnes Corporation's depot the same day, their No.4, one of six 56 seat all Leyland 'Titan' P1/1s new in 1946/1947, is immobilised without engine and wheels! It is being cannibalised to keep others in service.

No.27, a 1957 'Titan' PD2/12 with East Lancs 59 seat bodywork, passes the Corporation's depot. Note the odd front upper-deck windows which give a 'winking' effect.

No.18 in Widnes' fleet is one of two Leyland 'Royal Tiger' PSU1/13s with 44 seat Leyland bodywork, new in 1952.

In contrast, No.46 is a brand-new Leyland 'Panther' with dual entrance bodywork, just delivered to replace double deckers.

There could be no greater contrast than that between the new Leyland single decker seen above and this remarkable old timer which has survived as a towing vehicle for Widnes Corporation! It is No.69, one of three Leyland 'Lion' LT7s, with Massey bodywork, new in 1935. Survivors such as this were very rare indeed by 1967, luckily it survives in the care of the North West Museum of Road Transport today.

Next stop that day was Birkenhead, at whose Laird Street depot we see their No.23, a Massey bodied 61 seat Leyland 'Titan' PD2/40 new in 1959.

Also at the depot, No.193 is a 56 seat Massey bodied Guy 'Arab' III new in 1950 and now demoted to driver training duties. The use of the word 'Engaged' on its blind instead of the more usual 'Private' is somewhat odd!

I visited Wallasey Corporation again that day, too. Also now demoted to training duties, their No.37 is a Leyland 'Titan' PD2/1 with MCCW 56 seat bodywork new in 1951. It accompanies No.74, a PD2/12 with a Weymann 56 seat body new in 1952.

Across the Mersey at Liverpool Pier Head, Liverpool Corporation A191 is a 1958 AEC 'Regent' V with MCCW 58 seat bodywork and is about to depart for the by now immortalised Penny Lane. Note the unusual radiator grille for this type.

As London Transport did with a solitary 'Routemaster' and hundreds of Underground cars, Liverpool also tried buses in unpainted aluminium, albeit with a green window trim. One such is L307, a Leyland 'Titan' PD2/30 with 62 seat body built jointly by Crossley and the Corporation, seating 62.

Next stop that day was Wigan Corporation, who had also recently purchased high capacity, dual entrance Leyland 'Panther Cub' single deckers, in this case with Massey bodies. One of these, No.22, stands outside their depot.

No.81 provides an interesting comparison with the new 'Panther'. It is one of four Leyland 'Royal Tiger' PSU1/13s built in 1951 with 44 seat Northern Counties bodies. Note its unusual destination display!

Wigan No.159 represents the Corporation's older double deckers, being one of thirty all Leyland 56 seat 'Titan' PD2/1s new in 1950.

With very severe rear end damage, Wigan No.8, a 56 seat all Leyland 'Titan' PD2/12 built in 1953, has met premature withdrawal.

Wigan No.137 is seen at the terminus of the Corporation's route 2A in the town centre. It is a Leyland Titan PD3 with Massey bodywork.

Buses from the small Leigh Corporation fleet could also be seen in Wigan. The smartly turned out conductor of their 1957 East Lancs 58 seat lowbridge Leyland 'Titan' PD2/30 looks on as his driver adjusts its nearside wing mirror. Behind is a Lancashire United Daimler 'Fleetline'.

My destination that weekend was Blackpool for its illuminated trams. Early next morning, Sunday 10 September 1967, No.324 calls at Norbreck station on the seafront when bound for Fleetwood. It has Charles Roberts bodywork on Maley and Thompson trucks, with Crompton Parkinson equipment and was built in 1954.

On the way homewards, we called at Preston Corporation's depot. An odd survivor there is their No.75, one of two Leyland 'Tiger' PS1/1s with East Lancs 34 seat bodies new in 1949. It has recently been overhauled and painted in Preston's new blue and cream livery!

A real oddity in Preston's fleet is No.59, a Leyland 'Titan' PD2 recently rebuilt with a front entrance and lengthened! This work meant that it had to be re-registered with a new F-suffix registration. It also bears the new livery.

More mundane in Preston's fleet is No.24, a 58 seat Crossley bodied Leyland 'Titan' PD2/10 new in 1957 and carrying the older maroon and cream livery.

Our last call on the way back to London was Leigh Corporation's depot. Their No.41 is an East Lancs bodied 53 seat lowbridge AEC 'Regent' III new in 1953.

Leigh No.21 is a Leyland 'Titan' PD2/3 with Roberts 53 seat lowbridge bodywork new in 1951.

A very unusual vehicle in Leigh's small but varied fleet is No.60, one of four East Lancs 72 seat Dennis 'Loline' Is new in 1958/1959. The Birch Brothers Harrington 'Crusader' coach behind it is our means of transport to and from these operators that weekend.

A visit to Birmingham on 24 September 1967 finds two generations of the Corporation's buses at Washwood Heath garage: **No.2391, a** 54 seat Crossley with Crossley bodywork built in 1950, No.2481 of the same type and date but with 'tin front' and a 1966 Daimler 'Fleetline'.

A trip to Bradford on 7 October 1967 finds the Corporation's trolleybus No.841 passing Bradford Exchange station. This is a Sunbeam F4 that had been new to Mexborough & Swinton in 1950 with single decker bodywork, but after that system was abandoned, it was acquired along with others in its batch by Bradford Corporation and given the new East Lancs 69 seat body seen here in 1962. These were the last double deck bodies ever built for trolleybuses working in Great Britain. No fewer than four of this batch survive in preservation.

Beneath the wires at Thornbury depot, Bradford Corporation No.554 is one of twenty all Leyland 56 seat 'Titan' PD2/3s built in 1949.

Still in service is Bradford No.1, a 56 seat Weymann bodied AEC 'Regent' III new in 1949 as first of a batch of forty. It is seen in a depot which still has tram tracks!

Bradford Corporation had several AEC 'Regent' IIIs of a different kind – surplus 'RTs' acquired from London Transport in 1958. One of them, No.415 (ex-RT412) follows a trolleybus at Forster Square.

A newer 'Regent' III in Bradford's fleet is No.72, disguised with a 'tin front' radiator and carrying 59 seat East Lancs bodywork. It is one of forty built in 1952/1953.

With a West Riding Guy 'Wulfrunian' in the background, Bradford Corporation 1949 all Leyland 'Titan' PD2/3 56-seater No.48 heads for Adwalton. This is one of a batch of 25 supplied in 1949/1950.

Still with its original Weymann 59 seat bodywork, Bradford trolleybus No.753 is a BUT 9611T new in 1950, one of a batch of eight.

The last of the many visits I made to Birmingham was on 15 October 1967, when the Corporation's No. 1908, an MCCW bodied Daimler CVG6 54-seater built in 1949, is seen passing Midland Red's Digbeth coach station. By now, these vehicles were being rapidly withdrawn.

Now due for imminent withdrawal, Birmingham No.296 is a prototype all Leyland 'Titan' PD2 56-seater new in 1947. It is seen at Rosebery Street garage.

Another prototype for the Birmingham fleet is No.3246, their first Daimler 'Fleetline' with MCCW bodywork new in 1962. It is seen at Hockley.

Still going strong at Perry Barr garage is No.2245, one of thirty Leyland 'Tiger' PS2s with MCCW 34 seat bodywork new in 1950.

At the Corporation's Rosebery Street garage, No.2206 is one of fifty Leyland 'Titan' PD2s with Park Royal 54 seat bodies new in 1949/1950.

No.3432, one of Birmingham City transport's many Daimler 'Fleetlines', has suffered front end damage when seen here at Quinton garage.

Also at Quinton, Marshall bodied Bedford No.3660 represents a new generation of Birmingham vehicles.